Peeling The Earth Like An Onion

Earth Composition
Geology Books for Kids
Children's Earth Sciences Books

BABY PROFESSOR

EDUCATION KIDS

Speedy Publishing LLC
40 E. Main St. #1156
Newark, DE 19711
www.speedypublishing.com

We live on a ball of matter whizzing through the emptiness of space. But the Earth is not solid like a bowling ball. It has layers and layers, some solid and some molten, full of surprises. Read on and find out about what's under your feet!

Earth's Layers

There are two systems of naming the layers of the earth, as we go from the surface to the center. They are chemical variation and rheological differentiation.

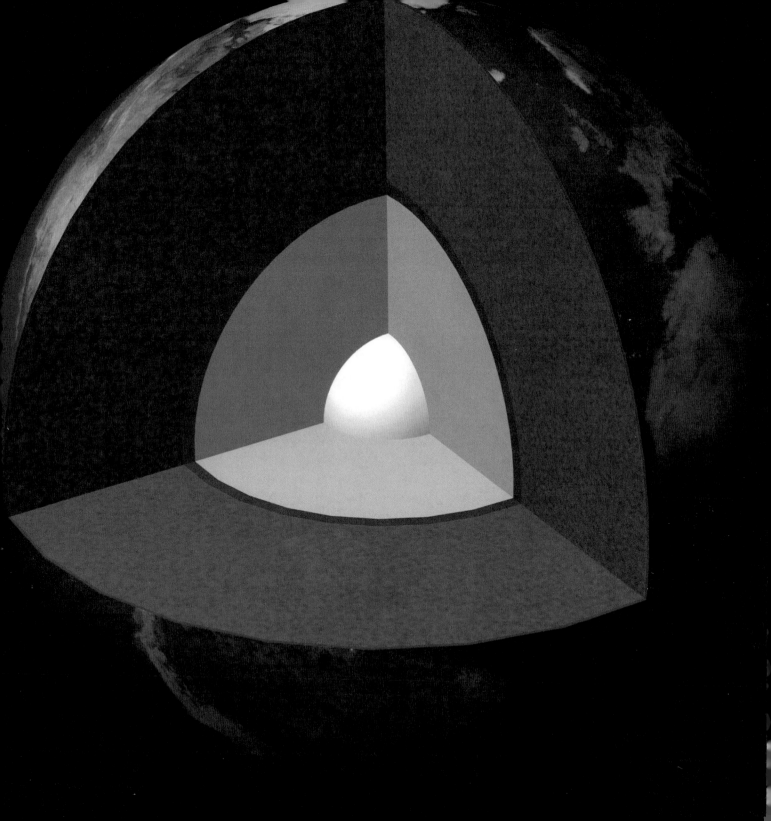

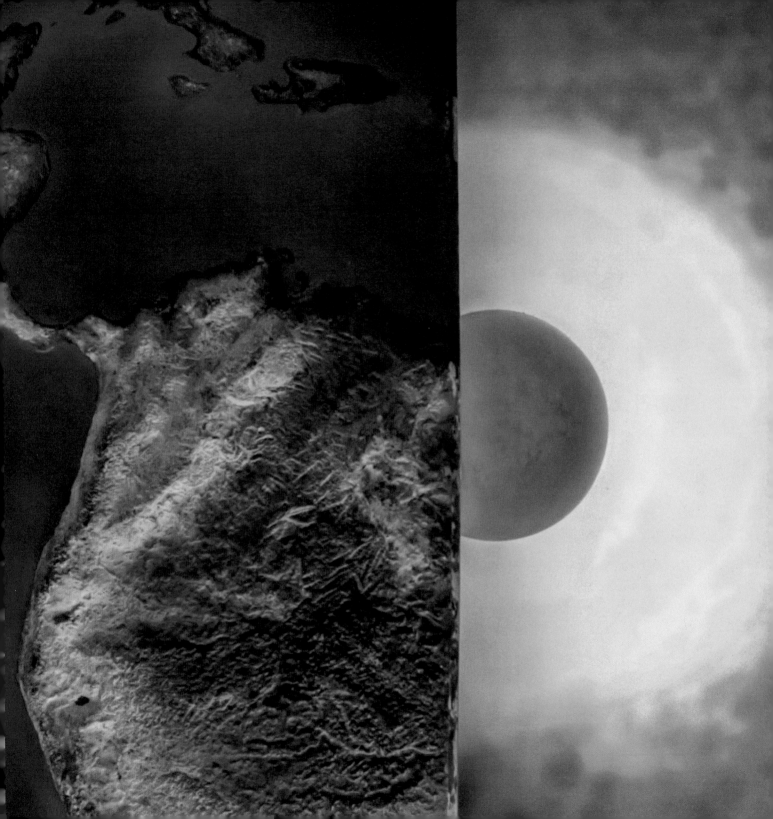

We'll follow chemical variation in this book. According to this system, our Earth has roughly four layers. Going from the outside in, they are the outer crust, the mantle, the outer core and the inner core.

The second system, rheological differentiation, evaluates the liquid state of rocks when they are under intense pressure and high temperatures. Generally, the further into the Earth you go, the higher both the pressure and the temperature rise. This system gives five layers instead of four. They are the lithosphere, asthenosphere, mesosphere, outer core and inner core.

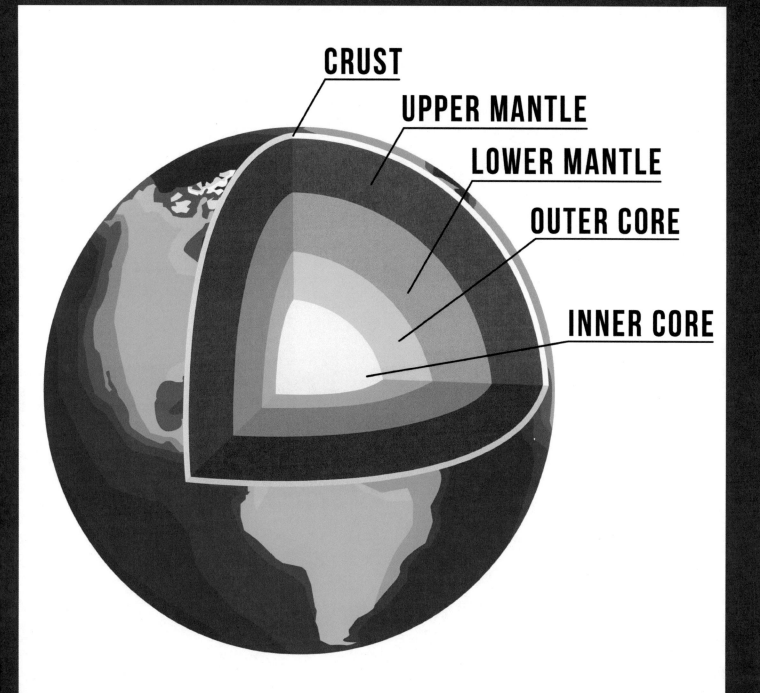

CRUST

UPPER MANTLE

LOWER MANTLE

OUTER CORE

INNER CORE

The Outer Crust

Here's where we live, you and I, out on the outer crust of the Earth. It feels very solid and it is, but where you're sitting reading this the top layer of the crust beneath you is probably only ten or 15 kilometers deep. If you are on a high mountain you could have as much as 50 kilometers of the top layer of crust underneath you.

The crust under the sea is both thinner and denser than the dry-land crust. The sea bottom crust is about five kilometers deep, but because it is denser it sinks lower down than the dry-land crust. The crust under the sea is largely basalt rock and the crust that makes up the continents has more rock like granite.

Earth's crust is actually a jigsaw puzzle of 17 huge puzzle pieces or plates. Together the 17 plates cover the whole Earth. But the plates are constantly pressing on and either moving toward or away from their neighbors. We aren't exactly sure how this got started, but at least we have a good name for what is happeninghappening, it is called "plate tectonics".

American

Eurasian Plate

P

African Plate

Arabian Plate

Indian Plate

South American Plate

Aus Pl

Scotia Plate

Antarctic Plate

The 17 plates are of dramatically different sizes and of course much of many of the plates are located under the oceans. The Arabian Plate is not much larger than the Arabian Peninsula and the countries of Jordan, Israel, Lebanon and Syria, which ride on it. Africa, by contrast, sits in the middle of the African Plate, which is more than three times the size of the continent it carries.

When two plates press toward each other they crumple together and the place where they meet gets higher. The Himalaya Mountain range is the result of the tectonic plate that India is on bashing into the south side of the Asia plate.

When two plates move away from each other material from the next layer down, the mantle, surges up to add new material to the crust. Iceland gains some land over time as it sits on top of a line where two tectonic plates are moving apart. This is where volcanoes appear too, as material from the mantle shoots up through the crust to make its presence felt.

When two tectonic plates slide along each other, rather than pressing toward or away from each other, the result can be earthquakes. Then, although the motion is small, the result can topple buildings and cause landslides and tsunami waves. The destruction can be terrible for animal and plant life.

These collisions and movements happen very, very slowly, but they have a long-term effect. Millions of years ago, when the dinosaurs were active, all the continents were connected to each other in one super-continent so you could travel to any continent without having to swim. Since then very slowly, the plates the continents sit on have moved into a new arrangement, the one we know from our maps.

Below the top layer of the crust, where the tectonic plates make the outer skin of the Earth, the crust has two more areas. A cooler layer and then a much hotter layer that is like a lubricant that helps the tectonic plates move. The cooler layer is about 100 kilometers thick, and the hotter layer is 700 kilometers thick.

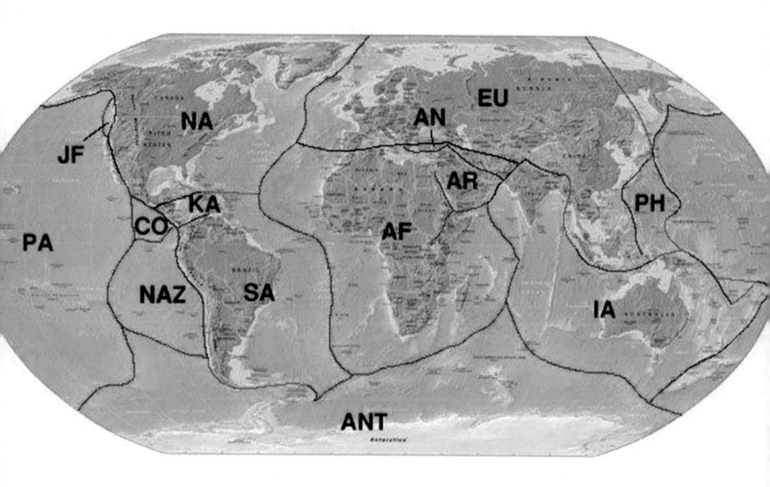

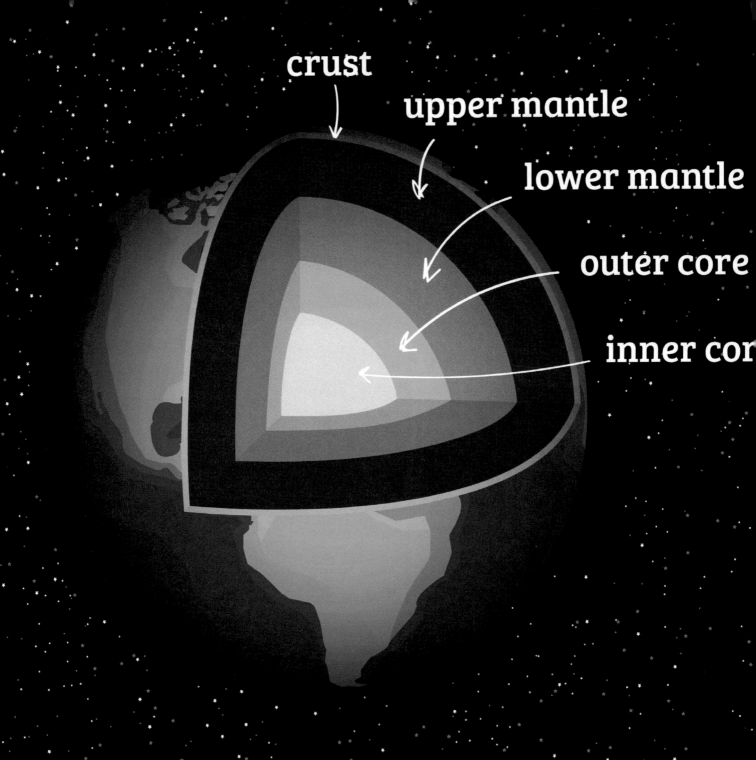

crust

upper mantle

lower mantle

outer core

inner cor

The Mantle

The mantle is the next layer in. It is much denser, softer and more flexible than the material of the crust and much, much hotter. It is hot enough to distort rock and so over long periods the mantle develops peaks that press up into and even through the crust.

The mantle is almost 3,000 kilometers thick. At its outer edge, its temperature is between 500 and 900 degress Celsius. At its inner edge, just above the outer core, the mantle reaches about 4,000 degrees Celsius. The mantle is the largest part of the Earth. It contains almost 85% of the Earth's volume.

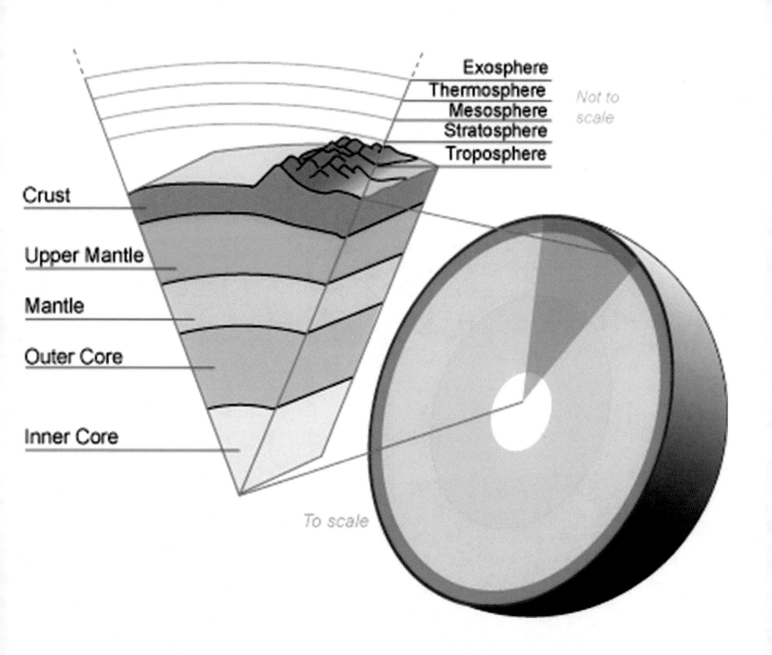

Exosphere
Thermosphere
Mesosphere
Stratosphere
Troposphere

Not to scale

Crust

Upper Mantle

Mantle

Outer Core

Inner Core

To scale

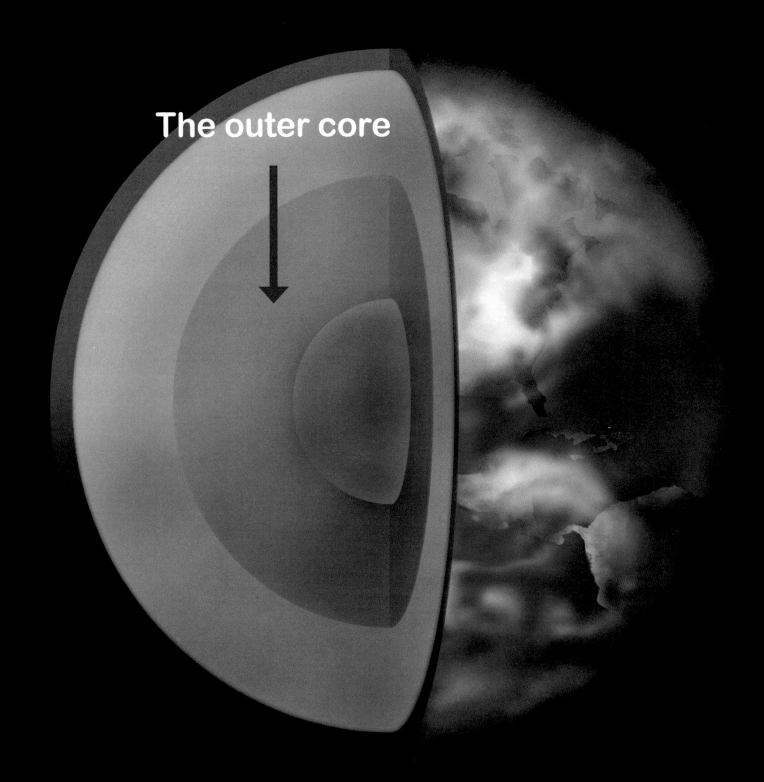

The Outer Core

The next layer on our way to the center of the Earth is the outer core. This layer is basically liquid iron, with some nickel and other elements, intensely hot and under extreme pressure. The outer core is about 2,300 kilometers thick.

When the Earth formed billions of years ago heavier elements tended to sink in toward the center, letting less dense elements move outward toward the mantle and the crust.

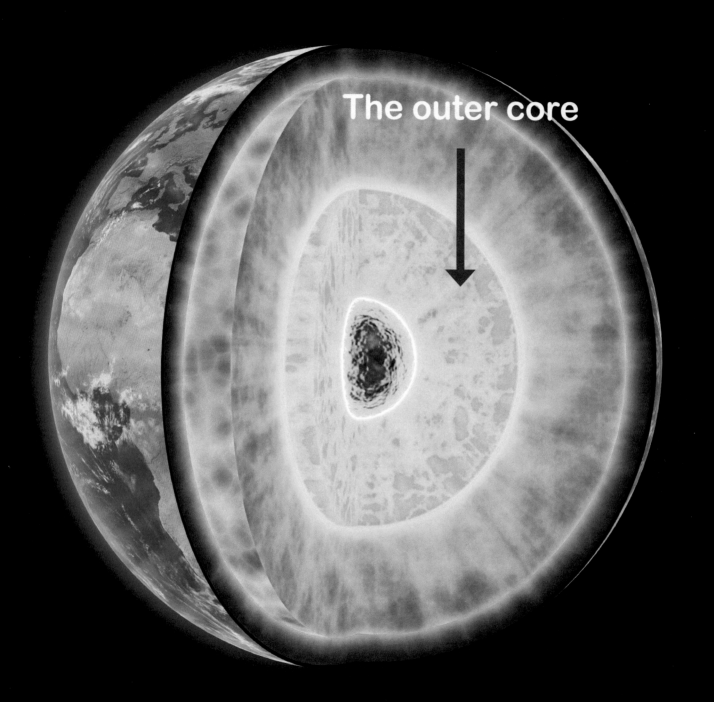

The outer core

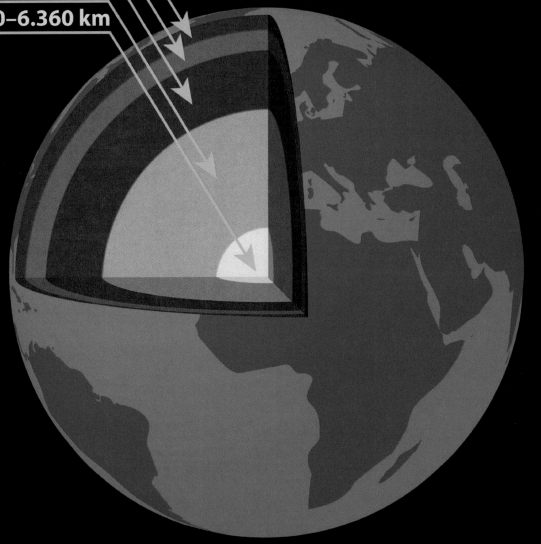

Crust 0-35 km
Upper mantle 35-60 km
Mantle 35–2.890 km
Outer core 2.890–5.150 km
Inner core 5.150–6.360 km

STRUCTURE OF THE EARTH

The temperature of the outer core is between 4,000 and 6,000 degrees Celsius. It is so fluid that it may spin faster than the Earth itself turns! This spinning helps create Earth's gravitational field.

The Inner Core

When we move from the outer core of our Earth to the inner core, we move to a zone of even higher heat and such great pressure that, despite the high heat, the inner core is solid. It is mainly iron and nickel with other heavy elements. Those include gold, silver, palladium, platinum and tungsten.

The outer core

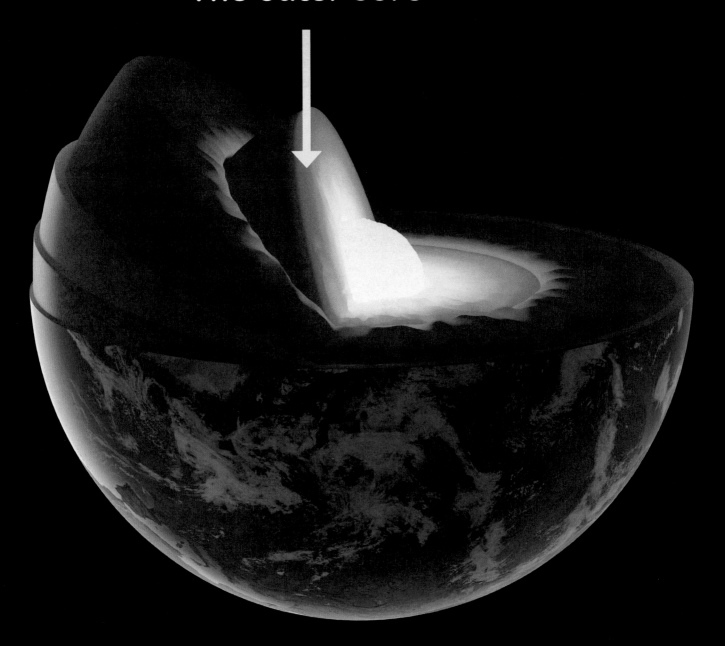

The outer core

The inner core of our planet is about 2,500 kilometers across. To give a sense of size, that's about two-thirds the diameter of our Moon. And the temperatures of the inner core get as hot as the temperature on the surface of the Sun!

Deep Mysteries

Needless to say, nobody has ever been to our planet's core or even into the mantle. The world's deepest mine, in South Africa, is less than four kilometers deep. You would need a shaft more than 15 times that deep just to get through the very outmost layer of the Earth's crust, if you start from dry land.

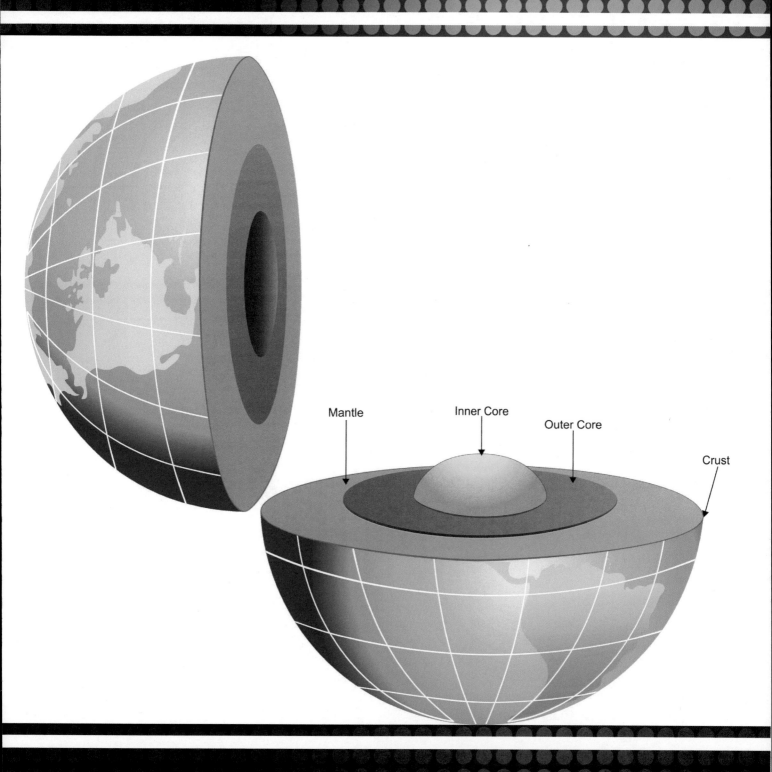

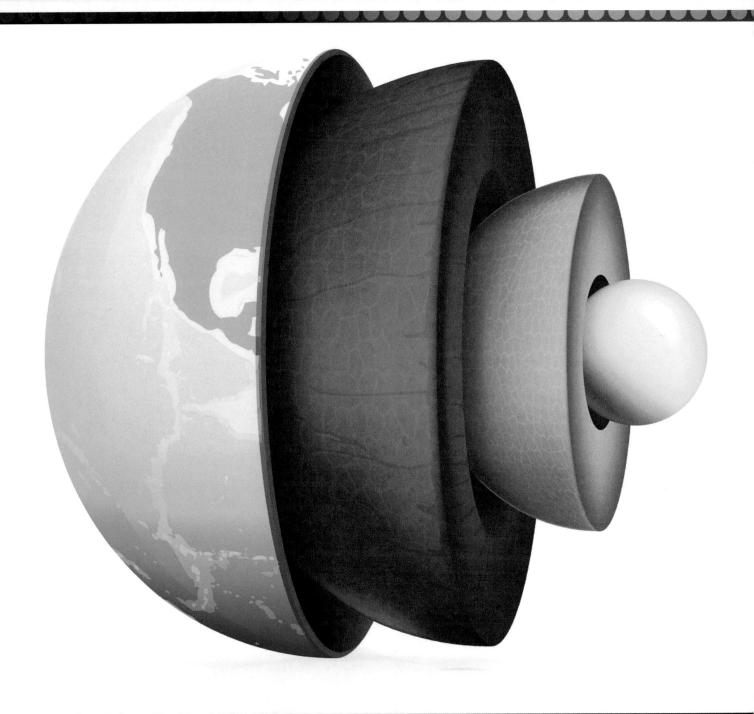

A project in 1961 tried to demonstrate that it would be possible to drill deep enough to penetrate through the bottom of the crust layer and take samples from the mantle, rather than waiting for volcanoes to provide them. Project Mohole sank six shafts off the coast of Mexico, working at a depth of more than 3,500 meters below the ocean's surface.

The project succeeded in drilling holes six hundred feet deep into the crust and brought up many valuable samples. However, the expense of going further was judged much too high for the possible benefits gained, especially as the United States was spending so much money at the time to get a man to the moon and the project was abandoned.

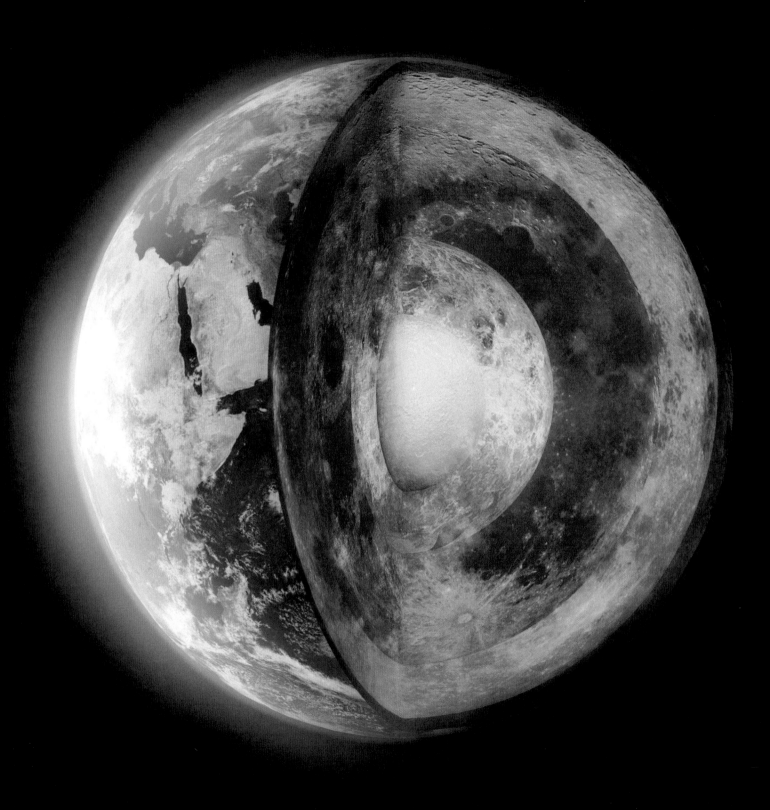

In 1692, scientist Edmond Halley suggested that the Earth must be be made up of several thick shells, with a hollow center 500 miles across. He was trying to account for the fact that measurements by Sir Isaac Newton seemed to suggest that the moon was more dense, overall, than the earth.

This theory gave rise to fantastical ideas about lost worlds hidden just below the furthest we could dig. So how do we know what's further inside our Earth? Scientists use various technologies, like studying seismic waves that pass through the Earth.

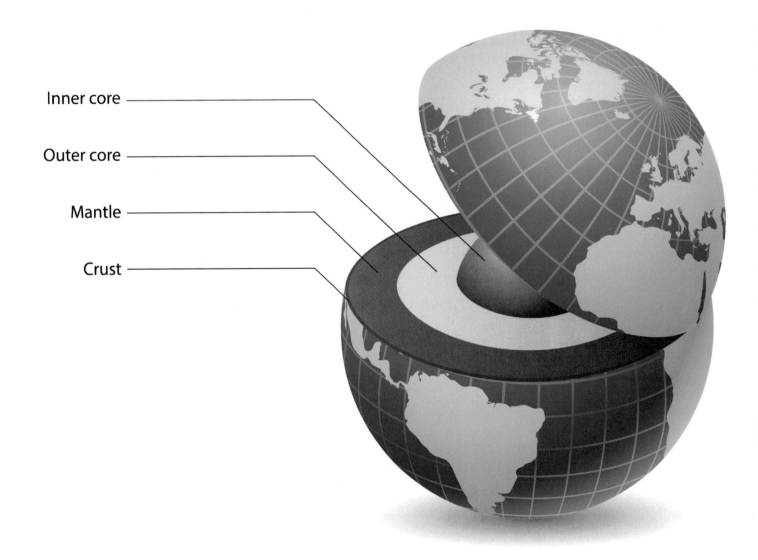

Inner core

Outer core

Mantle

Crust

They study rocks that volcanoes bring to the surface and measure changes in the Earth's magnetic and gravitational fields. In laboratories, they conduct experiments that try to simulate the high pressure and temperatures in the center of our planet, to learn their effects on rocks and minerals.

We know from studies of the Earth's gravitational field that its average density is just over 5,000 kilograms per cubic meter. Since the average density of the crust is around 3,000 kilograms per cubic meter, there must be much denser stuff further in.

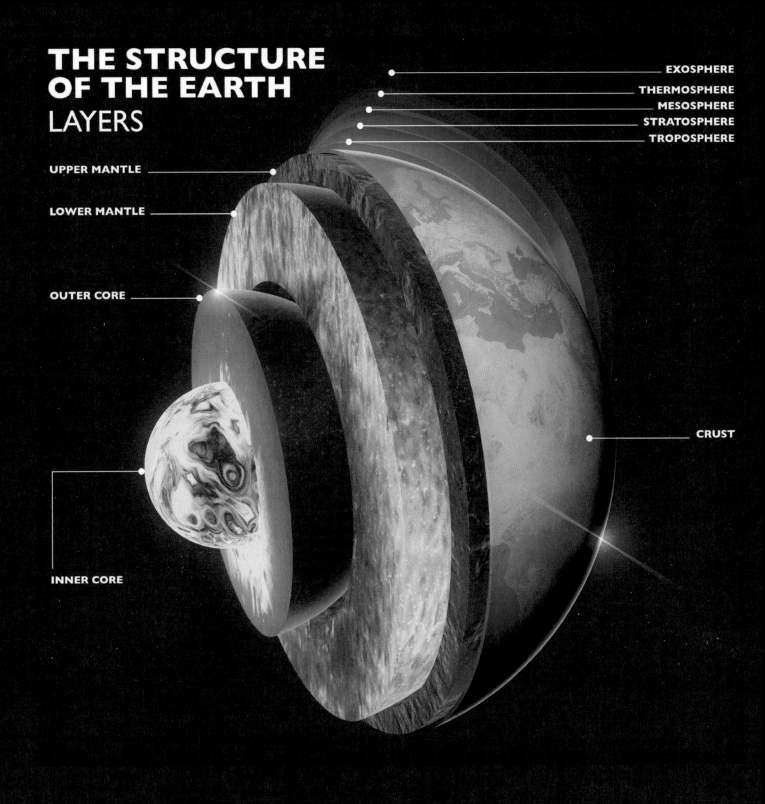

THE STRUCTURE OF THE EARTH
LAYERS

EXOSPHERE

THERMOSPHERE

MESOSPHERE

STRATOSPHERE

TROPOSPHERE

UPPER MANTLE

LOWER MANTLE

OUTER CORE

CRUST

INNER CORE

But the depths of the various layers and their temperatures, are based on the best possible scientific estimates. Nobody has ever stuck a thermometer into the mantle!

Basically, although the inner reaches of our planet are just a few thousand kilometers away, they are in many ways as hard to study and learn about as the other planets in our Solar Sytem are. We are still discovering what is going on in the interior of the Earth and the more we learn about our planet, the more we learn about other planets and about how everything in the universe came to be.

Our Wonderful Home, the Earth

Wherever you look, up at the sky, around at the plants and animals or down at the ground under your feet, there is more to learn about the Earth, our home. Read other Baby Professor books, like What Happens Before and After Volcanoes Erupt?, to learn more.

Visit

BABY PROFESSOR
EDUCATION KIDS

www.BabyProfessorBooks.com

to download Free Baby Professor eBooks
and view our catalog of new and exciting
Children's Books

Made in the USA
Monee, IL
10 August 2020